TRADE CAREERS
CARPENTER

by Joanne Mattern

Ideas for Parents and Teachers

Pogo Books let children practice reading informational text while introducing them to nonfiction features such as headings, labels, sidebars, maps, and diagrams, as well as a table of contents, glossary, and index.

Carefully leveled text with a strong photo match offers early fluent readers the support they need to succeed.

Before Reading

- "Walk" through the book and point out the various nonfiction features. Ask the student what purpose each feature serves.
- Look at the glossary together. Read and discuss the words.

Read the Book

- Have the child read the book independently.
- Invite him or her to list questions that arise from reading.

After Reading

- Discuss the child's questions. Talk about how he or she might find answers to those questions.
- Prompt the child to think more. Ask: Would you like to be a carpenter? What do you like about this trade career?

Pogo Books are published by Jump!
5357 Penn Avenue South
Minneapolis, MN 55419
www.jumplibrary.com

Copyright © 2025 Jump!
International copyright reserved in all countries. No part of this book may be reproduced in any form without written permission from the publisher.

Library of Congress Cataloging-in-Publication Data

Names: Mattern, Joanne, 1963- author.
Title: Carpenter / by Joanne Mattern.
Description: Minneapolis, MN: Jump!, Inc., [2025]
Series: Trade careers | Includes index.
Audience: Ages 7-10
Identifiers: LCCN 2023053332 (print)
LCCN 2023053333 (ebook)
ISBN 9798892131551 (hardcover)
ISBN 9798892131568 (paperback)
ISBN 9798892131575 (ebook)
Subjects: LCSH: Carpentry–Vocational guidance–Juvenile literature.
Classification: LCC TH5608.8 .M38 2025 (print)
LCC TH5608.8 (ebook)
DDC 694.023—dc23/eng/20231122
LC record available at https://lccn.loc.gov/2023053332
LC ebook record available at https://lccn.loc.gov/2023053333

Editor: Alyssa Sorenson
Designer: Anna Peterson
Content Consultant: Jeff Corning, Carpentry Instructor, Hennepin Technical College

Photo Credits: Francescomoufotografo/Shutterstock, cover; Nikola Ilic/Getty, 1; monticello/Shutterstock, 3; AmbientIdeas/iStock, 4 (left); Chatham172/Shutterstock, 4 (right); Trong Nguyen/Shutterstock, 5; Konstantin Gushcha/Shutterstock, 6-7; Orange Line Media/Shutterstock, 8-9; worradirek/Shutterstock, 10-11; Shutterstock, 11 (hammer), 11 (drill), 11 (tape measure), 11 (nails), 11 (level); naumoid/iStock, 11 (miter saw); Roman Kunitski/Dreamstime, 11 (nail gun); Ingram Publishing/SuperStock, 12; sturti/iStock, 13; anatoliy_gleb/Shutterstock, 14-15; simonkr/iStock, 16-17; ilkercelik/iStock, 18; Bilanol/iStock, 19; AnnaStills/iStock, 20-21; ifong/Shutterstock, 23.

Printed in the United States of America at Corporate Graphics in North Mankato, Minnesota.

TABLE OF CONTENTS

CHAPTER 1
What Is a Carpenter?.................................4

CHAPTER 2
Learning the Trade................................12

CHAPTER 3
Where They Work.................................18

ACTIVITIES & TOOLS
Try This!...22
Glossary...23
Index..24
To Learn More.....................................24

CHAPTER 1
WHAT IS A CARPENTER?

Carpenters work with wood and other materials. They build, **install**, and fix things. Their days often start early. They look at plans. Today, they are building a house!

plans

They build the house's frame. It is made of wood. It **supports** the house.

frame

CHAPTER 1

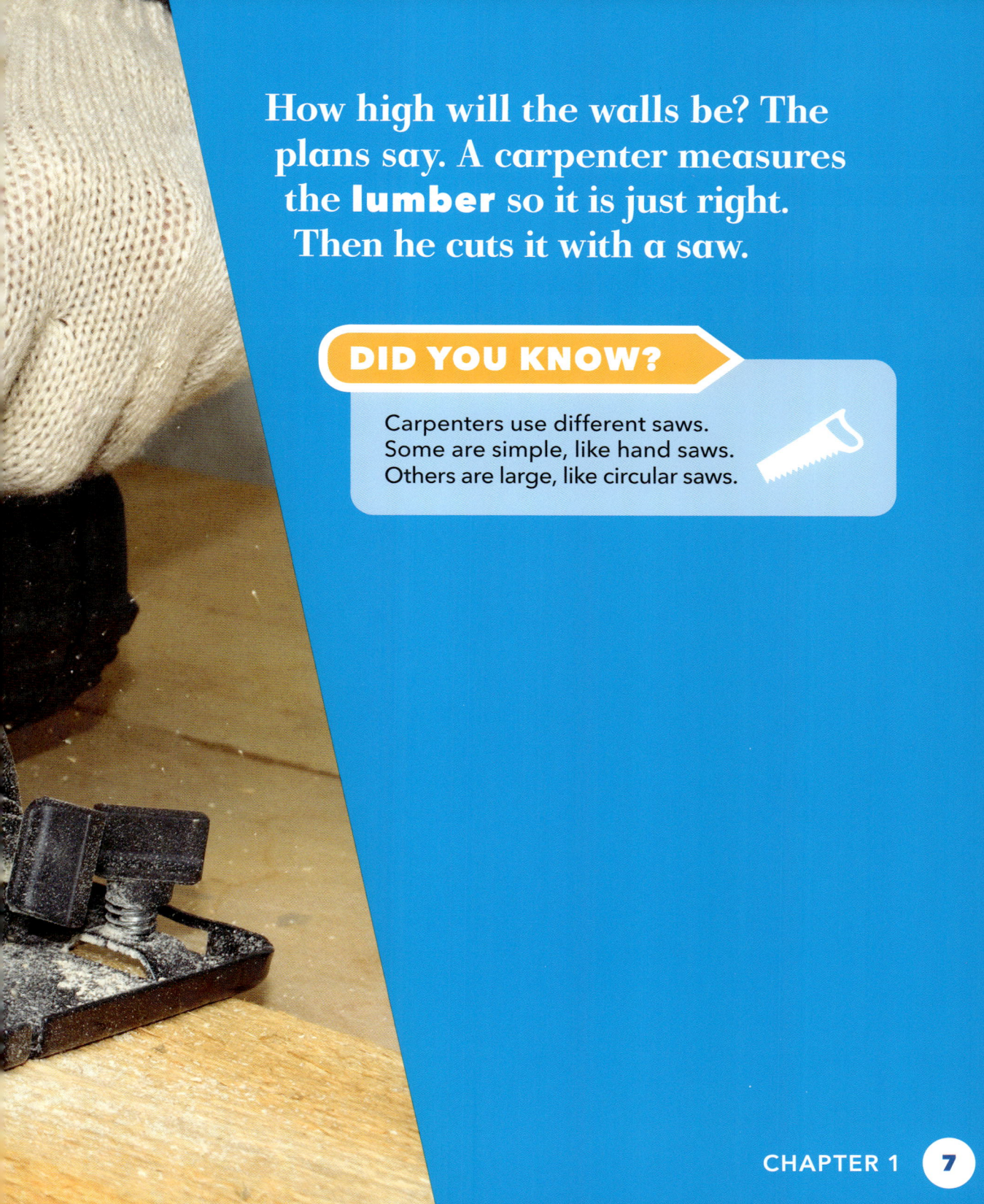

How high will the walls be? The plans say. A carpenter measures the **lumber** so it is just right. Then he cuts it with a saw.

DID YOU KNOW?

Carpenters use different saws. Some are simple, like hand saws. Others are large, like circular saws.

Carpenters nail pieces of lumber together. Everything is connected. Then what? Carpenters lift the frame. They put it in place. The walls take shape!

CHAPTER 1

CHAPTER 1

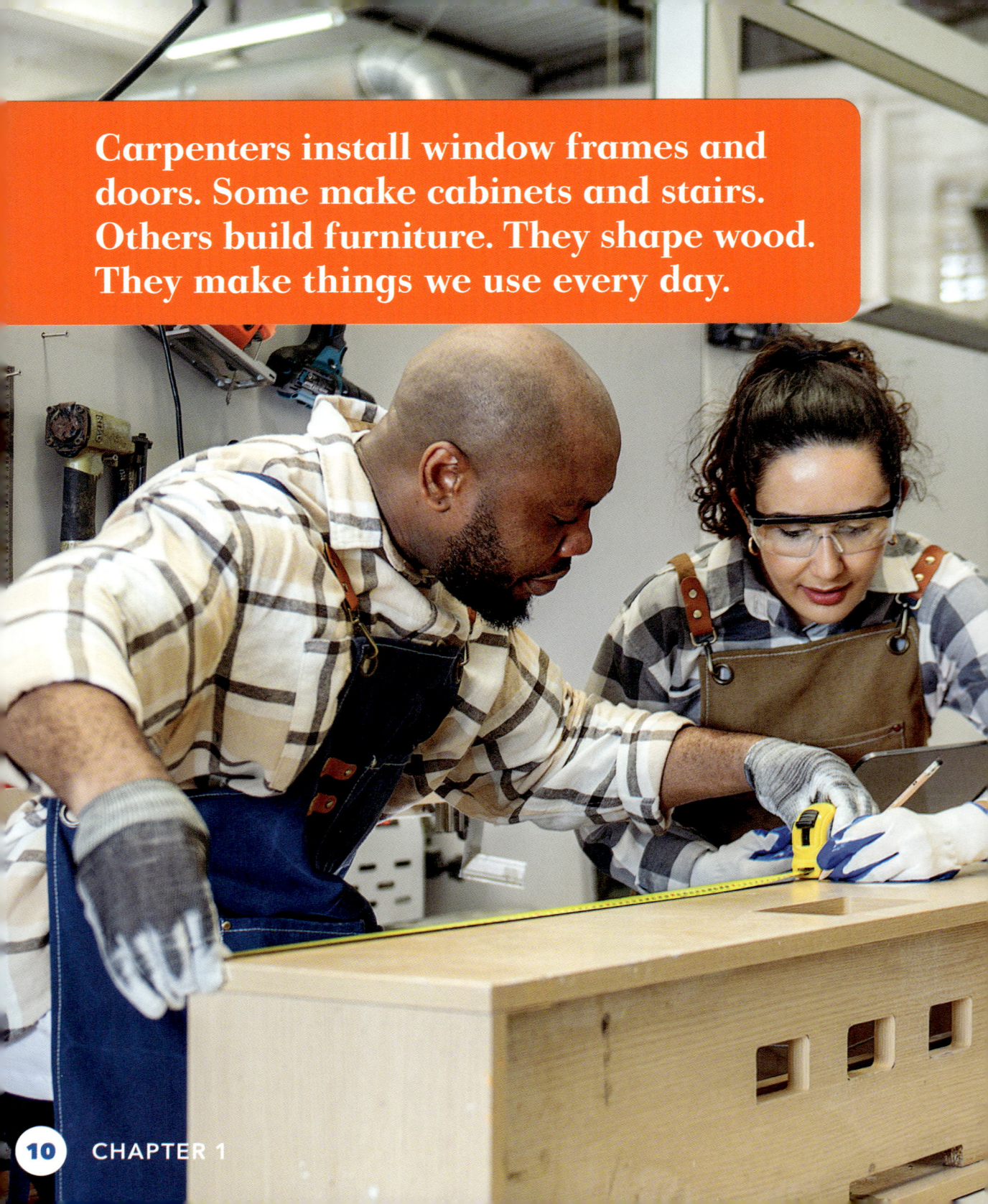

Carpenters install window frames and doors. Some make cabinets and stairs. Others build furniture. They shape wood. They make things we use every day.

CHAPTER 1

TAKE A LOOK!

What are some tools carpenters use? Take a look!

hammer: pounds nails in place

drill: makes holes

tape measure: measures how long something is

miter saw: cuts wood

nails: metal pieces that hold wood together

nail gun: shoots nails

level: makes sure a surface is exactly horizontal or vertical

CHAPTER 1　11

CHAPTER 2
LEARNING THE TRADE

Do you want to be a carpenter? You can take classes to learn the **trade**. Some high schools and community colleges have carpentry classes. **Vocational schools** teach carpentry, too.

People might do **apprenticeships**. They watch and learn from a carpenter who has a lot of experience. They may do this for three or four years.

apprentice

Carpenters measure a lot. They need good math skills. They should know **geometry** and **algebra**.

Carpenters pay close attention to details. Why? They have to make sure measurements are exactly right. Correct measurements make sturdy, safe objects.

DID YOU KNOW?

Carpenters often carry heavy objects. They bend and lift. They spend a lot of time on their feet. Their job is hard work!

CHAPTER 2   15

Carpenters often work together. They need good communication skills. Everyone on the job needs to know what to do. That way, they get the job done right.

Problem-solving is another important skill. Carpenters may have to figure out how to fix something. They solve problems to make sure everything is built right.

CHAPTER 2

CHAPTER 3
WHERE THEY WORK

Carpenters often work at construction sites. They build frames for houses, stores, and office buildings.

Carpenters also make and install floors, doors, and **trim**. They also put in **drywall** and **insulation**.

drywall

insulation

CHAPTER 3　19

Some carpenters are in workshops. They make furniture, such as tables and chairs. They also make bookcases or shelves. Some teach carpentry skills!

Carpentry is an important career. We need skilled workers to build things. There are many carpentry jobs. Would you like to be a carpenter?

DID YOU KNOW?

Some carpenters build and fix ships. They are called shipwrights.

ACTIVITIES & TOOLS

TRY THIS!

BUILD A PICTURE FRAME

Build a wooden picture frame in this fun activity!

What You Need:
- 4 Popsicle sticks
- glue
- paint and paintbrush
- markers
- beads
- tape
- photo

❶ Make a square with the Popsicle sticks.

❷ Glue the Popsicle sticks together. Wait for the glue to dry.

❸ Paint the Popsicle sticks. Wait for the paint to dry.

❹ Decorate the Popsicle sticks. You can write or draw on them with markers. You can glue beads onto the wood. Wait for the glue to dry.

❺ Tape a photo to the back of the Popsicle sticks. The image should face out of the frame. Now you have a picture frame!

GLOSSARY

algebra: The branch of math that deals with symbols and letters used to represent numbers.

apprenticeships: Arrangements through which people learn a trade by working with an expert.

drywall: Boards made of paper and plaster that are used to make ceilings and walls.

geometry: The branch of math that deals with points, lines, angles, and shapes.

install: To put something in place.

insulation: Material used to keep heat and sound from entering and leaving a building.

lumber: Wood that has been cut into pieces for building.

supports: Holds the weight of something.

trade: A job that requires working with the hands or with machines.

trim: A material, such as wood, that surrounds openings like windows and doors.

vocational schools: Schools that prepare students for jobs in trade careers.

INDEX

apprenticeships 13
cabinets 10
classes 12
communication 16
community colleges 12
construction sites 18
drywall 19
frame 5, 8, 18
furniture 10, 21
install 4, 10, 19
insulation 19
lumber 7, 8
math 15
measures 7, 11, 15
nail 8, 11
plans 4, 7
problem-solving 16
saw 7, 11
shipwrights 21
tools 11
vocational schools 12
window frames 10
wood 4, 5, 10, 11
workshops 21

TO LEARN MORE

Finding more information is as easy as 1, 2, 3.
1. Go to www.factsurfer.com
2. Enter "carpenter" into the search box.
3. Choose your book to see a list of websites.